WORLD
OF
BIRDS

NATIONAL WILDLIFE FEDERATION'S

WORLD
OF
BIRDS

A BEGINNER'S GUIDE

KIM KURKI

BLACK DOG
& LEVENTHAL
PUBLISHERS

This book is dedicated, with love, to my parents,
who had to call me in from the outdoors by ringing a bell
and encouraged me to follow my dreams:
to my mom, Grace, whose unconditional support made this
possible, and to my dad, Lauri, who would have been so proud.

—Kim "Lizbird" Kurki (my dad's nickname for me)

ISBN: 978-1-57912-969-9

Library of Congress Cataloging-in-Publication Data on file at the offices of Black Dog & Leventhal Publishers, Inc.

Manufactured in China

Published by Black Dog & Leventhal Publishers, Inc. 151 West 19th Street New York, New York 10011

Distributed by Workman Publishing Company 225 Varick Street New York, New York 10014

h g f e d c b a

CONTENTS

FIELDS, THICKETS & BACKYARDS

WOODLANDS & FORESTS

WETLANDS, SHORES & BODIES OF WATER

DESERTS, SCRUBLANDS & ROCKY SLOPES

INTRODUCTION

Whenever I'm asked, "If you could be any animal, what would you be?" my answer is always "a bird." Ever since I was a child, I thought it would be so cool to be able to fly, soaring on the wind and getting a "bird's-eye view" of my neighborhood and the surrounding wild places. When I was a young artist, my dad encouraged me to "paint something bright." One of my first bird paintings was a cardinal. I've been painting the natural world ever since.

Lucky for me, I had the chance to pursue this passion when I worked for National Wildlife Federation's *Your Big Backyard* magazine for almost a decade. In each of my monthly columns, titled "Explore the Big Outdoors," I spotlighted fascinating facts about a bird, animal, plant, or insect that children might find in their own backyard. *World of Birds* grew out of that column and I'm glad it did. From my treetop studio, I have compiled a collection of some of the most common and interesting birds around the world.

Among the fun and amazing facts about our feathered friends, you'll learn in this book about the biggest and the smallest bird, the fastest flier and the deepest diver. You'll read about their songs, their calls, how they attract mates, where they live, and what their nests are like. There are birds that eat only fish, and some that eat mainly insects or seeds. But other birds eat almost everything, including dead animals.

DID YOU KNOW

that a male and female Bald Eagle will mate for life, and each year, they build a new nest on top of the old one? It may be as large as 9½ feet (3 m) wide by 20 feet (6 m) high. One nest was reported to weigh nearly two tons (1,816 kg).

The **BALD EAGLE** was chosen as the official national symbol of the United States in 1782. It's named for the striking white feathers on its head, giving it the appearance of baldness.

Some birds would rather swim than walk, some birds would rather walk than fly, and some birds run very fast!

Even with my years of experience, I still found many of the birds surprising. Who knew a puffin's brightly colored beak peels off after the breeding season? Or that the bold roadrunner won't think twice about attacking and eating a poisonous rattlesnake? If the snake is too long, the roadrunner will eat what it can and then walk around with the other end of the snake hanging out of its mouth until it can digest the whole thing.

My hope is that, by reading *World of Birds,* you experience the joy I get spotting a huge Pileated Woodpecker hammering in a tree or watching a couple of wrens flit back and forth as they build their nest. Maybe then you'll go outside and find the birds that live near you. You'll listen for the hooting owl at night, watch for the bright-yellow finches in your garden, and witness the V-shape flight of the Canada geese as they honk and flap in the autumn sky. I hope you have fun exploring nature's winged wonders with which we share our world.

BIRD HABITAT

The birds in each full-page profile are grouped by habitat, or the area where they are most often found. Each bird's habitat varies based on its needs. For example, the Greater Sage-Grouse eats mainly sage, so it lives where the sagebrush grows. That is a very specific habitat in the Desert, Scrublands, & Rocky Slopes chapter.

Other birds, like the Herring Gull, eat a wide variety of food and can be found in many different habitats all over the world. However, most often they make their home by the water, so in this book they appear in the Wetlands, Shores & Bodies of Water chapter.

FIELDS, THICKETS & BACKYARDS

WETLANDS, SHORES & BODIES OF WATER

The book is divided into four common habitats:

FIELDS, THICKETS & BACKYARDS

Birds found in this chapter live in both natural fields and on farms; in backyards in both the cities and suburbs; and in thickets, which are groups of bushes or small trees that grow close together.

WOODLANDS & FORESTS

Birds found in this chapter live in or among trees, in both dense and open forests.

WETLANDS, SHORES & BODIES OF WATER

Birds found in this chapter live in wetlands, such as swamps or marshes; on pebbly or sandy shores along oceans, seas, or lakes; or near other bodies of water, including brooks, rivers, and streams.

DESERTS, SCRUBLANDS & ROCKY SLOPES

Birds found in this chapter live in open areas that don't get a lot of rain. They live among cacti and shrubby thickets, with few trees.

DESERTS, SCRUBLANDS & ROCKY SLOPES

WOODLANDS & FORESTS

IDENTIFYING BIRDS

The goal of this book is to celebrate the mind-boggling variety of birds in the world. However, if you are looking at two similar birds, how do you tell them apart?

Here are a few things to consider:

PLUMAGE

The color of the feathers of a bird is the easiest identifier. Some are easy to spot, such as the bright-yellow body of the Golden Oriole. Others are more subtle, like the shimmer of color on an otherwise black Grackle. Also, the male and female of a species often look different, with the male generally being more brightly colored, so I've pointed out where that occurs.

From the tiny Hummingbird to an Ostrich taller than a person, a bird's size depends on its species. If you know the average size of a bird, you can help identify it. For example, ravens and crows look very similar. Both birds are totally black, with large, heavy bills. However, ravens are much bigger than crows, so knowing the size helps.

SIZE

If you can get close enough to a bird, you can learn a lot about it just by looking at its feet, beak, or bill. The structure varies depending on what the bird eats and where it lives. For example, a Mallard Duck has webbed feet to paddle around a pond and uses its flat bill to collect water plants. Meanwhile, a Pileated Woodpecker has a long, pointed bill for making holes in trees to reach insects. It also has curved claws to help it cling to tree bark.

FEET, BEAK & BILL

Some birds are named for their common call, such as the Blue Jay's "jay" call, which helps you identify them by sound. Others, like the Northern Mockingbird, have many songs and even imitate other birds, so it easier to identify them by sight. Even birds that rarely use their voice often make other noises, like a Turkey Vulture that hisses and grunts.

While this book is not a traditional field guide, it does provide a great introduction to more than 100 birds, highlighting their amazing habits and traits. Enjoy your adventure into the wondrous world of birds!

SCARLET SONGSTER

THE MALE IS THE ONLY CRESTED RED BIRD IN THE U.S.

NORTHERN CARDINAL

CHOSEN BY SEVEN STATES IN THE U.S. AS THEIR OFFICIAL BIRD.

FOUND IN BACK-YARDS, THICKETS, AND MEADOWS FROM CANADA TO AS FAR SOUTH AS BELIZE.

ITS SHORT, THICK BILL CAN CRACK OPEN HARD SEEDS.

ALSO KNOWN AS REDBIRD

MALE

FEMALE

A cardinal on a winter day
Shines like a ruby through the gray.
With bright red feathers, pointed crest,
This bird stands out from all the rest.

A treat to see and also hear,
It might break out in song all year.
It does not migrate, does not roam,
Far from the place it calls home.

IN SPRING, THE MALE WILL FEED HIS MATE AS SHE SITS ON THE NEST.

AT FEEDERS SUNFLOWER SEEDS ARE FAVORITES.

IN THE WILD IT EATS MOSTLY SEEDS AND BERRIES, BUT ALSO SOME INSECTS.

HE WILL ALSO CARE FOR THE YOUNG WHILE THE FEMALE NESTS AGAIN.

Constant Chorus

Both the male and female are excellent singers. They might be heard at any time of the year, not just in spring when most other birds sing.

HOME SWEET HOME

Once they move into your yard, a cardinal family may live there for many years.

Imaginary Foe

A male will fiercely defend his feeding territory. You may see him fighting his reflection in a car mirror or window, trying to scare off the "other" bird.

HOUSE FINCH

MALE FEMALE

PURPLE FINCH

MALE

FEMALE

Bird-Feeder Buddies

Other reddish birds will commonly be seen sharing time with cardinals at bird feeders in North America. Like the cardinal, these finches are seed eaters, which you can tell by their short, thick bills.

PYRRHULOXIA

Has a crest →

Also known as Desert Cardinal, it is found in the southwestern U.S. and Mexico.

13

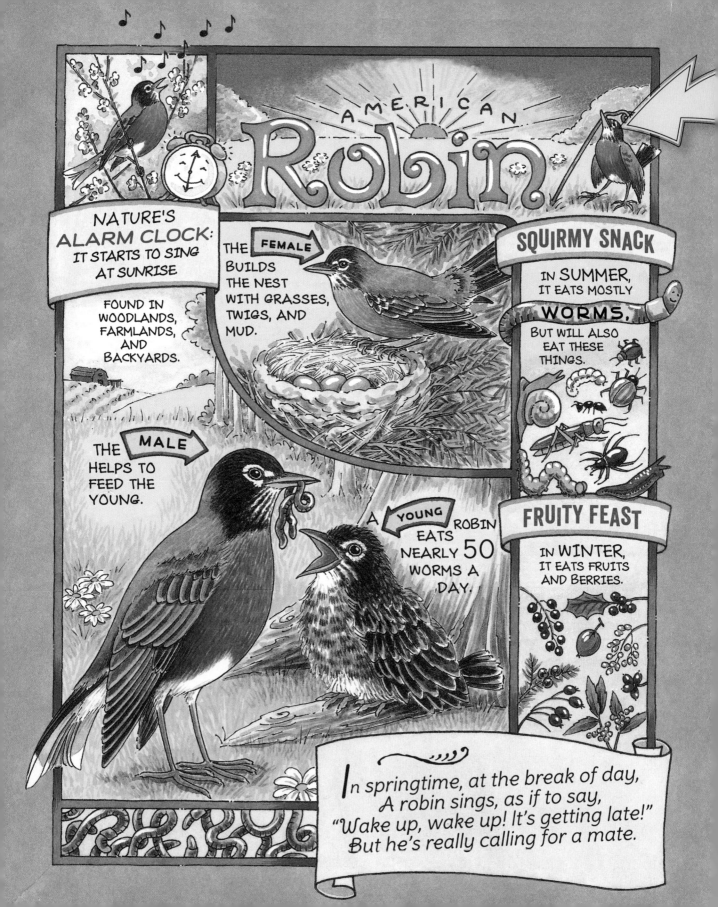

AMERICAN Robin

NATURE'S ALARM CLOCK: IT STARTS TO SING AT SUNRISE

FOUND IN WOODLANDS, FARMLANDS, AND BACKYARDS.

THE **FEMALE** BUILDS THE NEST WITH GRASSES, TWIGS, AND MUD.

THE **MALE** HELPS TO FEED THE YOUNG.

A **YOUNG** ROBIN EATS NEARLY 50 WORMS A DAY.

SQUIRMY SNACK

IN SUMMER, IT EATS MOSTLY **WORMS,** BUT WILL ALSO EAT THESE THINGS.

FRUITY FEAST

IN WINTER, IT EATS FRUITS AND BERRIES.

In springtime, at the break of day,
A robin sings, as if to say,
"Wake up, wake up! It's getting late!"
But he's really calling for a mate.

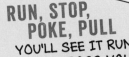

RUN, STOP, POKE, PULL
YOU'LL SEE IT RUNNING ACROSS YOUR LAWN, STOPPING TO SNATCH A WORM.

Cocking its head from side to side, it seems to be listening for worms. Actually, it spots them by sight and pulls them from the ground.

It eats **68** worms a day, or **14** feet of worms laid end to end, as many as **15** worms an hour.

Take a Second Look

EASTERN TOWHEE
(Its call sounds like its name.)
Often mistaken for a robin. However, a towhee is smaller and has a mostly white breast with reddish patches on the sides.

MALE

FEMALE

Like a robin, the female is paler.

Also known as GROUND ROBIN

You will probably hear the towhee before you see it, as it scratches noisily for insects in dry leaves, under shrubs, and in thickets, where it hides.

Bon Voyage

Although they are traditionally seen as a first sign of spring, they are common year-round throughout much of the United States.

Robins generally migrate short distances, especially those in Canada and Alaska.

EUROPEAN ROBIN

A favorite of bird lovers in western Europe, this birds is about half the size of an American Robin. Both the male and female look alike, with a bright orange breast.

15

Blue Tit

GREAT TIT

EUROPEAN ROBIN

EURASIAN NUTHATCH

BACKYARD BUDDIES

A COMMON VISITOR TO FEEDERS, THIS LIVELY TIT IS OFTEN SEEN WITH OTHER BIRDS.

FEMALE

THE FEMALE MAY BE SLIGHTLY PALER THAN THE MALE.

MALE

THE NAME TIT IS SHORTENED FROM THE ORIGINAL NAME TITMOUSE, GENERALLY MEANING "SMALL BIRD."

IT NESTS IN TREE CAVITIES, ABANDONED WOODPECKER HOLES, AND NEST BOXES.

FEEDING FRENZY

IT HAS A LARGE FAMILY OF 7-16 CHICKS. EACH NESTLING WILL EAT ABOUT 100 CATERPILLARS A DAY.

*Blue Tits flying back and forth
To bring their nestlings lots of food
Can make a thousand trips a day
With caterpillars for their brood.*

THE BLUE TIT HOLDS THE RECORD FOR THE MOST EGGS LAID BY A SONGBIRD IN A SINGLE NEST — 19!

The Blue Tit is a familiar small bird across much of Europe, North Africa, the Middle East, and parts of Asia. It's found mainly in woodlands, but is also common in open habitats, such as parks and gardens.

Gardener's Friends

In summer, the Blue Tit eats mostly aphids, a pest that can damage plants. It will hang upside down to find aphids under leaves.

Rat-a-Tat Crack

In winter, the Blue Tit eats mostly seeds and nuts. It will hold a nut with its feet or wedge it into a crevice to hammer it open with its bill.

CATERPILLAR CLEANUP
SOME CATERPILLARS MAY BITE OR INJURE NESTLINGS. THE PARENT BIRD WILL BREAK THE JAWS AND REMOVE POISONOUS PARTS OF A CATERPILLAR BEFORE FEEDING IT TO ITS YOUNG.

American Cousins

The **BLACK-CAPPED CHICKADEE** and the Tufted Titmouse are both members of the Tit family. They are found in eastern North America and share many nesting and feeding habits with the European Tits. Found mainly in woodlands, these friendly birds are also familiar sights at feeders. The Black-capped Chickadee may become quite tame and can learn to eat from your hand. It's named for its call, which sounds like "schick-a-dee."

The **TUFTED TITMOUSE** has a "tuft" or crest of feathers on it head. It lines its nest with fur, sometimes plucked from living animals.

Topsy-Turvy

A common companion to these birds at feeders is the **WHITE-BREASTED NUTHATCH**. Also known as "upside-down birds," White-breasted Nuthatches creep down tree trunks headfirst, looking for insects in bark crevices. With their strong feet, they also walk upside down on small branches.

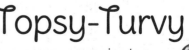

17

House Wren

ALSO KNOWN AS THE JENNY WREN

LIVES NEAR HOUSES, FARMS, AND BRUSHY WOODS IN NORTH AND SOUTH AMERICA.

HOME SWEET HOME

WRENS BUILD NESTS IN MANY ODD PLACES . . .

AND IN HOUSES MADE JUST FOR THEM.

WRENS EAT **LOTS** OF INSECTS.

The House Wren sings a bubbly song
While gathering twigs the whole day long.
He's busy building several nests.
His mate will choose the one that's best.

Busy, Noisy Builder

A male will sing his gurgling song throughout the nesting season.

He will return to the same nesting place each spring and start to build as many as a dozen nests.

He will fill up any suitable nook with sticks and may use up to 500 sticks in a single nest.

These practice nests are called "dummy nests." The female will choose the one she likes and will help to finish it.

Both parents feed the young. A single pair may make 600 food-carrying trips in a single day.

Bully Bird

Although it's otherwise a delight, a wren may invade nests of other birds to defend its territory. It will puncture and remove eggs from sites where it wants to nest.

More Backyard Bluster

A native of Europe, much of Asia, and part of the Mediterranean, the **HOUSE SPARROW** has been introduced throughout the world and resides where humans live.

FEMALE

MALE

This noisy and aggressive bird will steal nest sites (such as this bluebird box) from native hole-nesting birds (including wrens).

EXTENDED FAMILY

The **CAROLINA WREN** is found mainly in the eastern United States. It is larger than the House Wren and has white stripes above its eyes.

CACTUS WREN

This large wren builds stick nests among the spines of a cactus in Mexico and the southwestern United States.

EASTERN Bluebird

HOME SWEET HOLE

THEY BUILD NESTS INSIDE HOLES IN:

- **TREES**
- **FENCE POSTS**
- **BOXES** MADE JUST FOR THEM

FOUND IN OPEN WOODLANDS AND MEADOWS FROM SOUTHERN CANADA TO AS FAR SOUTH AS NICARAGUA IN CENTRAL AMERICA.

MALE

FEMALE

THE BLUEBIRD IS A SYMBOL OF **HAPPINESS** AND **LUCK**.

IN WINTER THEY EAT LOTS OF WILD BERRIES.

THEY EAT MANY INSECTS **IN SUMMER**.

A flash of blue feathers will catch your eye
As a brilliant bluebird swoops nearby.
A cheery call will comfort your ear.
Its sweet, soft song is a treat to hear.

The Return of the Bluebirds

Decades ago, this peaceful bird was not as common as it is today. Aggressive nonnative birds such as starlings and House Sparrows were taking over its nesting sites.

Concerned bird lovers built many nest boxes. They placed them facing open fields, where insects are easy to find. The perfect box for a bluebird has a 1½-inch (3.8 cm) opening, too small for starlings. If House Sparrows move in, human "bird helpers" remove the nesting materials.

Snug Shelter

On a frigid winter night, as many as a dozen bluebirds may huddle together in a tree cavity or nest box.

Farmers' Friend

The Bluebird eats many insects that can damage crops. Often seen perching on a fence post near farms, it will scan the ground and swoop down to grab its meal.

Upland Cousin

MALE

Like the Eastern Bluebird, the **MOUNTAIN BLUEBIRD** eats many insects, but it searches for them by hovering in the air. It either catches them in flight or drops down to pluck them from the ground.

It is found in high mountains, grasslands, meadows, and woodlands in western North America.

FEMALE

EUROPEAN Goldfinch

ALSO KNOWN AS THISTLE FINCH

MAGICAL MUSIC

KNOWN FOR THEIR ENCHANTING, SWEET SONG, A GROUP OF GOLDFINCHES IS CALLED A *CHARM*. THAT'S AN OLD-FASHIONED TERM FOR "MAGIC SONG" OR "SPELL."

THE **FEMALE** HAS LESS RED ON HER FACE THAN THE MALE.

THE GOLDFINCH RELIES ON THISTLES FOR FOOD. THE SEEDS ARE A FAVORITE AND THISTLE DOWN IS NEEDED TO LINE ITS NEST.

IT ALSO EATS THE SEEDS OF OTHER FLOWERS, GRASSES, AND WEEDS.

AGILE ACROBAT

IT CAN CLING TO NARROW STEMS AND DELICATE SEED HEADS, SOMETIMES UPSIDE DOWN.

THE GOLDFINCH HAS A LONG, FINE BILL TO PROBE FOR SEEDS.

MALE

LATE SEASON NESTER

WHILE MANY BIRDS NEST IN THE SPRING, THE GOLDFINCH WAITS UNTIL SUMMER, WHEN SEEDS AND PLANT DOWN ARE PLENTIFUL.

*By the yellow flash of its fluttering wings
And the silvery twittering as it sings,
You'll recognize this feathered gem
As it flits and flies from stem to stem.*

The European Goldfinch is found in Europe, North Africa, and parts of Asia. It has been introduced to other countries, including New Zealand, where previously there were no native finches.

Captive Caller

For many centuries, the European Goldfinches have been kept as cage birds because of their beautiful song and appearance.

Singing Lesson

Birds raised in captivity are very tame, but must learn to sing properly from other goldfinches.

Variations on a Theme

The males are sometimes cross-bred with canaries to combine the best singing aspects of both breeds. The resulting males are prized for their singing ability.

CHARM OF LOVE AND MONEY

A legend says that on Valentine's Day, if the first bird a girl sees is a goldfinch, she will marry a wealthy man.

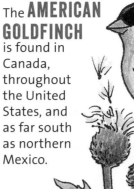

The **AMERICAN GOLDFINCH** is found in Canada, throughout the United States, and as far south as northern Mexico.

MALE

Also known as "Wild Canary" because of the male's bright yellow feathers and canary-like song.

Like the European Goldfinch, it relies on the thistle as an important source of food and nesting material. It nests late in the season, when flowers have gone to seed.

FEMALE

IN MICHIGAN, GOLDFINCH NESTS WITH EGGS HAVE BEEN FOUND AS LATE AS SEPTEMBER 25, WHICH IS RARE FOR BIRDS.

AMERICAN Kestrel

ALSO KNOWN AS

SPARROW HAWK

EATS MOSTLY MICE AND GRASSHOPPERS

FEMALE

MALE

OFTEN PERCHES ON TELEPHONE POLES, WIRES, FENCE POSTS, AND TREE LIMBS, SEARCHING FOR FOOD.

KESTREL KOPTER

IT HOVERS LIKE A HELICOPTER BEFORE IT POUNCES ON ITS PREY.

A KESTREL IS THE SIZE OF A BLUE JAY.

Perched above a grassy field,
A kestrel looks for prey.
It can spot a tasty meal
One hundred feet away.

HUNTING HABITS

A KESTREL WILL ZOOM DOWN AT HIGH SPEED TO GRAB ITS PREY ON THE GROUND, THEN CARRY IT OFF TO A FEEDING PERCH.

MASTER MOUSER

It may eat

290

mice in a year.

IT WILL ALSO EAT:

Nesting Nooks

Kestrels will nest in a tree cavity or an abandoned woodpecker hole. If trees are scarce, they will use a nest box built just for them.

Not a Hawk

While it is known as the "Sparrow Hawk" and eats small birds, the kestrel is not a hawk. It's the smallest and most common falcon in North and South America. A falcon's wings are longer and narrower than a hawk's wings.

Fleet Flyer of the Falcon Family

CITY SLICKER

A Peregrine Falcon will nest on a high building ledge. It is drawn to the city by the abundance of pigeons, a favorite food. Highly adaptable, the peregrine is one of the most widely distributed birds of prey, found on all continents.

The **PEREGRINE FALCON** swoops down on prey with a powerful dive called a "stoop," plunging at up to 200 miles (322 km) per hour. The force of impact on its prey in midair normally stuns or kills it.

Also known as "Duck Hawk," it will eat many birds, including pigeons, shorebirds, and large birds such as ducks.

25

WILD TURKEY

FOUND IN OPEN WOODS AND FIELDS

WILD TURKEY WAS PLENTIFUL WHEN THE PILGRIMS CAME TO AMERICA.

BENJAMIN FRANKLIN THOUGHT THE WILD TURKEY SHOULD BE THE UNITED STATES'S NATIONAL BIRD.

THE WILD TURKEY IS FOUND IN ALMOST EVERY STATE IN AMERICA.

A Wild Turkey's gobble
Can be heard a mile away.
He fans his tail and struts his stuff
In a colorful display.

He wags his bright red wattle
While puffing out his breast
To show approaching females
That he clearly is the best.

SEARCHES BY DAY FOR ACORNS, BERRIES, INSECTS, AND CORN

ROOSTS IN TREES BY NIGHT

All-American Bird

The Wild Turkey is native to North America, where it is the largest game bird. That means it is hunted for sport. Native Americans introduced it to the first settlers as a good source of food.

Chinese Cousin

The **RING-NECKED PHEASANT**, a native of Asia, was brought to North America for game hunting more than 100 years ago.

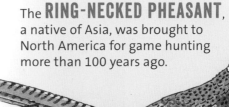

PATRIOTIC DISPLAY

The male's head turns red, white, and blue when he's ready to mate.

This puffy, loose skin is the "wattle."

The Ring-Necked Pheasant's tail is as long as or longer than its body.

Toms' Turkey Trot

The males, called "toms," will parade around to attract females, called "hens." A hen will choose just one mate, but a tom will mate with several hens.

THE FAMILIAR "GOBBLE-GOBBLE" IS THE MALES' MATING CALL.

Courting Cock

A male pheasant, called a "cock," will crow to claim territory. He crows every three to five minutes, for about an hour.

His beautiful feathers help him attract females, called "hens."

HIDEAWAY NEST

The hen builds a nest on the ground with dead leaves and grass where she can blend in with her surroundings.

Ground Nester

The hen scrapes out a nest from dirt and leaves. She calls softly to the chicks inside the eggs, maybe to let them know when it's time to come out. The chicks can find their own food soon after hatching.

BEAUTIFUL BIRD

The **OCELLATED TURKEY**, only found in the Yucatan Peninsula of Mexico, has beautiful shimmering feathers.

RED-TAILED HAWK

SOAR AND SWOOP
IT RIDES THE AIR LIKE A SAILING KITE.

MEATY MENU
IT EATS MOSTLY **MICE** AND **RATS**,

BUT WILL ALSO EAT THESE SMALL ANIMALS:

SUPER SIGHT

FROM A HIGH PERCH, IT SCANS THE GROUND FOR FOOD.

*You'll hear its whistling cry
And spot its tail of red
As this graceful, gliding hawk
Circles overhead.*

SOARING

IS WHEN A HAWK GLIDES THROUGH THE SKY ON RISING AIR CURRENTS. THIS SKILL MEANS IT CAN FLY FOR LONG PERIODS WITHOUT FLAPPING ITS WINGS.

Aerial Hunters

This hawk has eyesight up to eight times keener than that of humans. Both the Red-tailed Hawk and the Osprey can spot their prey from the air, and both have razor-sharp talons to seize their catch. The Red-tailed Hawk captures its prey on the ground. The Osprey snags its meal from the water.

HAWK family member

The **OSPREY** is a kind of hawk. Like the Red-tailed Hawk, the Osprey soars. It has been observed soaring at 80 miles (129 km) per hour.

LOFTY ROOST

Both of these birds build a large nest of sticks and twigs. The Red-tailed Hawk builds it high up in a tree. The Osprey will also build it in a tree or on top of a telephone pole or a channel marker.

ALSO KNOWN AS "FISH HAWK," THE OSPREY IS THE ONE RAPTOR (BIRD OF PREY) THAT EATS ONLY FISH.

Love in the Air

Male and female Red-tailed Hawks will call to each other and perform a dramatic acrobatic dance in the sky before mating.

The Red-tailed Hawk is one of the most common hawks in the United States. The Osprey is found throughout the world.

GREAT HORNED OWL

HUNTS AT NIGHT FOR RATS, MICE, AND OTHER SMALL ANIMALS.

ITS "HORNS" ARE FEATHERY TUFTS THAT LOOK LIKE EARS.

ITS EAR HOLES ARE HIDDEN UNDER FEATHERS NEAR ITS EYES.

IT LAYS EGGS IN A TREE NOOK OR AN OLD NEST OF A SQUIRREL OR LARGE BIRD.

SILENT IN FLIGHT

From high up in a frozen perch,
An owl calls its mate to start the search
For a spot to raise their little ones.
A new owl family has begun.

When winter snow is still on the ground,
At night, you may hear this curious sound.
The who-who-hoot of a Great Horned Owl
Says, "This is where I'm nesting now."

The Great Horned Owl is the most widely distributed owl in North and South America. It nests in forests, deserts, swamps, and even city parks.

THE HOOTING DUET OF PAIRED ADULTS IS ONE OF THE MOST FAMILIAR OWL CALLS.

MALE

The Hunter is the Hunted

The **BARN OWL** could become a midnight snack for a Great Horned Owl, but this smaller owl is quite a skillful hunter itself. This "flying mousetrap" has asymmetrical earholes (see arrows) that allow it to pinpoint the rustling of a mouse in total darkness.

ALSO KNOWN AS A "MONKEY-FACED OWL," IT HAS A DISTINCTIVE HEART-SHAPED FACE.

FEMALE

Moonlight Master Hunter

The Great Horned Owl hunts at night using its excellent hearing and keen vision. As its eyes do not move, it can turn its head 3/4 of the way around to see in all directions. It swoops silently to sneak up on prey.

MIDNIGHT MUNCHIES
RATS ★ MICE
RABBITS ★ FROGS
LIZARDS ★ SNAKES
OPOSSUMS
PORCUPINES
SMALL BIRDS
OTHER OWLS
TURKEYS ★ GEESE
AND EVEN
SKUNKS!!!

Telltale Leftovers

You might find owl pellets under a tree where the owl rests during the day. After eating, it coughs up a fuzzy lump of fur, teeth, bones, and feathers that its stomach can't digest.

Rodent Raider

The Barn Owl's name refers to its habit of nesting in barns, where mice are often plentiful. It is found almost everywhere in the world, outside of polar and desert regions.

an owl pellet

31

PILEATED WOODPECKER

PILEATED (PIE-lee-ay-tid) MEANS IT HAS A POINTED TUFT OF FEATHERS ON ITS HEAD.

THE LARGEST WOODPECKER IN NORTH AMERICA

MALE

ITS STRONG BILL HELPS IT DIG INTO AND CHIP WOOD.

YOU MAY FIND WOOD CHIPS AT THE BASE OF A TREE WHERE IT HAS BEEN FEEDING.

CURVED CLAWS HELP IT CLING TO TREE BARK.

FEMALE

"LOVE SONG"

A MALE WILL TAP AND DRUM ON A BRANCH TO ATTRACT A MATE.

SEARCH AND SNATCH

ITS LONG STICKY TONGUE CAN GRAB INSECTS DEEP WITHIN A TREE.

You'll probably hear it before you see
A woodpecker hammering on a tree.
Pecking at wood is what it does best.
It can dig to find insects or carve out a nest.

Under Cover Up High

Despite its large size and striking appearance, the Pileated Woodpecker is shy and keeps out of sight. You are more likely to hear it than see it.

ITS FEEDING HOLE IS LARGER THAN ITS NEST HOLE, AND IT'S EASIER TO FIND.

Safe, Secret Nest

This woodpecker will carve out its nest hole in a tree, 50–60 feet (15–18 m) above the ground. It will fly off with the wood chips to make the site less obvious.

INSECT DETECTOR

This woodpecker eats mostly insects and grubs. The wood-boring Carpenter Ant is a favorite. The bird can hear and see them under the bark of trees. It hammers and chisels with its bill to reach them. It grabs them with the barbed end of its tongue.

The woodpecker's **TONGUE** is so long that it wraps around the inside of its skull. It can extend three times the length of its bill.

It can slam its head against wood 100 times a minute.

FEEDER FRIENDS

The **DOWNY WOODPECKER** and the **RED-BELLIED WOODPECKER** are familiar sights at backyard feeders.

MALE

MALE

They can be attracted with suet cakes, made from beef fat and seed.

FEMALE

FEMALE

The Downy is the smallest woodpecker in North America. Don't confuse it with the Hairy Woodpecker, which has the same coloring but is much larger with a longer bill.

The Red-Bellied gets its name from the pale reddish patch of feathers on its lower abdomen, which is often hard to see.

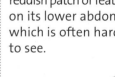

BLACK WOODPECKER

Distant Cousin

The Black Woodpecker is found in forests throughout most of Europe and northern Scandinavia and parts of northern Asia and the Middle East.

Ruffed Grouse

LIVES IN FORESTS

NAMED FOR THE BLACK "RUFFS" OF FEATHERS ON ITS NECK.

SNUG SHELTER

IT EATS MANY KINDS OF **PLANTS** AND SOME INSECTS.

MALE

IT OFTEN SLEEPS UNDER THE SNOW.

THE **FEMALE'S** RUFFS ARE SMALLER.

LOVE BEAT

EACH SPRING THE MALE "DRUMS" THE AIR WITH HIS WINGS TO ATTRACT A MATE.

The male Ruffed Grouse has a special way
To bring a mate around.
He beats the air with his whirring wings
To make a drumming sound.

Wild Chicken

The chicken-like Ruffed Grouse, found in North America, has feathers that can be rusty red (left page) or gray. It's often called a "partridge" in some parts of the country and is highly prized as a game bird.

Arctic Cousin

The **WILLOW PTARMIGAN** is a pigeon-sized grouse that lives in the frigid north of Europe, Scandinavia, Canada, China, Russia, and Alaska. It is named for its favorite winter food, the buds and twigs of a willow, which it digs for in the snow.

Clever Camouflage

Each season the Willow Ptarmigan changes color by growing new feathers to blend in with its surroundings. In winter, both male and female are snowy white. In summer, they are earthy browns.

Quick Getaway

A shy ground-dweller, the Ruffed Grouse stays hidden in the brush. When a predator comes close, it suddenly takes off with a noisy whirring of wings.

The grouse develops comb-like bristles on its toes that help keep it from sinking into the snow.

CRAZY COURTSHIP

WHEN THE MALE IS READY TO MATE, HE STANDS ON A LOG, DISPLAYS HIS FEATHERS, AND STARTS HIS MATING CALL. IT IS NOT A SONG OR A CRY, BUT RATHER A DEEP THUMPING THAT SPEEDS UP INTO A WHIRRING SOUND THAT CAN BE HEARD A MILE (1.5 KM) AWAY!

Winter Ways

Both the Ruffed Grouse and the Willow Ptarmigan burrow into snow for shelter. They also grow their own "snowshoes."

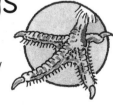

The ptarmigan grows feathers on its feet that help it to walk on top of newly fallen snow.

EURASIAN MAGPIE

MAGPIE MAGIC

AN OLD ENGLISH RHYME DETAILS THE FOLKLORE THAT YOU CAN PREDICT THE FUTURE BY COUNTING THE MAGPIES YOU SEE. "ONE FOR SORROW, TWO FOR MIRTH . . ."

THE **MALE** AND **FEMALE** LOOK ALIKE, BUT THE MALE'S TAIL MAY BE LONGER.

DANGER!

ALSO KNOWN AS ROBBER BIRDS

MAGPIES STEAL FOOD FROM FARMS, PEOPLE, AND OTHER ANIMALS, AND RAID THE NESTS OF OTHER BIRDS TO EAT THEIR EGGS AND YOUNG.

MAJOR MUNCHER

THOUGH INSECTS ARE A FAVORITE, MAGPIES EAT ALL KINDS OF FOOD, INCLUDING DEAD ANIMALS AND SCRAPS FROM HUMAN GARBAGE.

TASTY TIDBITS

MAGPIES EAT TICKS OFF SHEEP AND CATTLE.

HOME WITH A DOME

THEY BUILD A BULKY NEST OF STICKS, TOPPED WITH A CANOPY OF THORNY TWIGS. THE ENTRANCE IS HARD TO FIND.

A squawking magpie will call an alarm
When a predator is near to do it harm.
The magpie mob will save the day.
They'll pester the foe 'til it goes away.

The common Eurasian Magpie is a member of the family that includes crows, ravens, and jays. It is found in Europe, much of Asia, and northwestern Africa. It lives in woodlands, open areas, and gardens.

Magpie Mastermind

HI, HANDSOME!

The magpie is one of the most intelligent birds. It is the only bird known to recognize itself in the mirror. Noisy, chattering birds, magpies have been taught to mimic human speech.

Magpie Mourning

Magpies seem to express the human emotion of grief. They will gather around a dead magpie and chatter as if giving speeches. Then they all fly off in silence.

Magpie Myth

Magpies are thought to steal, collect, and hide shiny objects, such as keys and coins. Although this may occur when magpies are kept as pets, in the wild these curious birds will pick up and examine objects such as sticks and stones to determine if they are food. The only thing they do steal is food, and they may hide it in the ground to eat later on.

The bold and brash **AMERICAN CROW** is found throughout North America. Its familiar "caw caw" is heard in open woodlands, farmlands, parks, and suburbs.

Mischievous Mob

Like magpies, crows will gang up on a predator to chase it away. If you see a mob of crows harassing a larger bird, you might get a glimpse of a hawk or an owl.

Mob or Be Mobbed

In turn, smaller birds, such as a Red-winged Blackbird, will pester a crow to keep it away from its nest.

FARMER'S FRIEND OR FOE?
LIKE THE MAGPIE, A CROW WILL EAT ALMOST ANYTHING IT CAN SWALLOW. IT DAMAGES CROPS BY EATING ENORMOUS AMOUNTS OF GRAIN, BUT IT ALSO CONSUMES MANY HARMFUL INSECT PESTS.

Much larger than the crow, the raven is found throughout most of the Northern Hemisphere, but often in remote areas away from humans. Its black plumage and habit of eating dead animals have given rise to legends portraying this bird as evil or as a sign of doom. The captive ravens at the Tower of London, though beloved, are a little feared. Legend has it that, if they ever leave the tower, the British Empire will crumble.

COMMON RAVEN

37

EURASIAN
Golden Oriole

THE NAME **ORIOLE** COMES FROM A LATIN WORD MEANING "YELLOW" OR "GOLDEN."

TREETOP TUNES

THE MALE HAS A BEAUTIFUL SONG THAT SOUNDS LIKE A CLEAR FLUTE WHISTLE. ONCE YOU HEAR IT, YOU WON'T FORGET IT.

FEMALE

THE **MALE** DOES NOT SHARE IN NEST BUILDING, BUT WILL HELP INCUBATE THE EGGS AND FEED THE YOUNG.

MALE

HEARD, BUT NOT SEEN

SHY TREE DWELLERS, THEY HIDE AWAY IN THE HIGH BRANCHES. DESPITE THE MALE'S BRIGHT COLOR, HE AND THE DRAB FEMALE BLEND IN WITH THE DAPPLED LEAVES.

THE ORIOLE'S NEST IS SLUNG LIKE A HAMMOCK BETWEEN TWO FORKED BRANCHES. THE FEMALE WEAVES IT WITH STRIPS OF GRASS AND BARK.

TREETOP TIDBITS

THIS ORIOLE PRIMARILY EATS INSECTS IT FINDS IN TREES. CATERPILLARS ARE A FAVORITE. THE HAIRY ONES ARE BEATEN AGAINST BRANCHES TO REMOVE MOST OF THE HAIRS BEFORE BEING SWALLOWED.

When it comes to weaving a sturdy nest,
The female oriole is one of the best.
The fragile-looking, sack-like form
Hangs tight through almost any storm.

Orioles are found across mainland Europe into Asia and northwestern Africa, where they winter. Because these orioles make their homes high up in the tree canopy of forests and woodlands, you may catch a glimpse of the male's striking plumage only when he flies in the open.

Feathered Protector

This small bird will fiercely defend its territory when breeding, attacking birds as large as magpies.

Love in the Air

The female will start the courting ritual by flying by the male. He will then chase her in and out of the tree canopy, flying so close that his bill almost touches her tail.

Not All Orioles Are Orioles

Although it shares the name, the **BALTIMORE ORIOLE** is not related to the Golden Oriole. It is a member of the blackbird family. The Baltimore Oriole is the most common oriole in eastern North America. As with Golden Orioles, the male Baltimore Oriole is an outstanding songster, and the female weaves a hanging, pouch-like nest.

In winter, the Baltimore Oriole migrates **2,000** miles to South America and may return to the same tree in the North each spring.

WESTERN MEADOWLARK

Related to the Baltimore Oriole, this bird is not a lark but a member of the blackbird family. It lives in grasslands in middle to western North America. As a popular songbird, the male's enchanting song is heard as he sings on a visible perch.

Mourning Dove

THE MOURNING DOVE IS NAMED FOR ITS SOFT COOING, BUT THE MALE'S SAD, SWEET CALL IS REALLY A LOVE SONG. IT IS SOMETIMES MISTAKEN FOR THE CALL OF AN OWL

THESE GENTLE, AFFECTIONATE BIRDS ARE BELIEVED TO MATE FOR LIFE.

LABOR OF LOVE

THE FEMALE BUILDS A FLIMSY NEST IN A TREE OR SHRUB WITH TWIGS COLLECTED BY THE MALE. THE PAIR TAKES TURNS SITTING ON THE NEST.

THIS DOVE IS A POPULAR GAME BIRD, BUT IN SOME AREAS IT IS PROTECTED AS A SONGBIRD.

FEEDING FLUID

BOTH PARENTS FEED THE YOUNG WITH "PIGEON MILK," A LIQUID PRODUCED IN THEIR CROPS. THE CHICK POKES ITS BILL INTO THE PARENT'S MOUTH.

ITS **WINGS** AND **TAIL** MAKE A WHISTLING SOUND DURING FLIGHT, ESPECIALLY WHEN THE BIRD TAKES OFF.

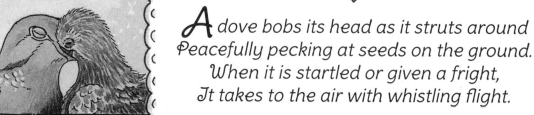

A dove bobs its head as it struts around
Peacefully pecking at seeds on the ground.
When it is startled or given a fright,
It takes to the air with whistling flight.

Familiar Feathered Friend

The Mourning Dove is common in North and Central America. There are 350 million of these birds in the United States. They are found everywhere except in deep woods and swamps.

Seed Saver and Stone Swallower

This dove searches for seeds and grain on the ground and can store thousands in its crop. It swallows gravel to help "grind" and digest the seeds in its gizzard.

CROP

GIZZARD

Splash-and-Sip Seeker

If the Mourning Dove is not nesting near water, it will fly long distances to drink and bathe. Travelers in the desert have learned to follow the flights of doves to find a water source.

BACKYARD BATH AND BEVERAGE

You can attract Mourning Doves to your yard by providing water, such as a bird-bath or a small pond. Unlike most birds, a Mourning Dove drinks water by sucking it into its bill, rather than lifting its head to let the water run down its throat.

Cooing Cousin

Doves and pigeons belong in the same family. Though it is not always the case, pigeons tend to be larger and have shorter tails, while doves are smaller with longer pointed tails.

Downtown Digs

The **ROCK PIGEON** is commonly found in cities throughout the world.

Its wild ancestor, the Rock Dove, still nests in the high, rocky cliffs of Europe. The pigeon is comfortable nesting on high ledges of city buildings. Like Mourning Doves, a pair mates for life and feeds the young with "pigeon milk."

Home Sweet Homing Pigeon

Pigeons are able to find their way home no matter where they are. This ability is known as "homing." For thousands of years, people have used these birds to carry messages over long distances. These so-called "carrier pigeons" were used extensively in World Wars I and II. Some even received medals for service.

PASSENGER PIGEON

The Passenger Pigeon was once the most abundant bird in North America. With flocks of up to a billion birds, the pigeon became extinct due to over-hunting and loss of habitat. The last Passenger Pigeon in the world, named Martha, died in 1914 at the Cincinnati Zoo.

SCREECH OWL

ITS "SCREECH" IS ACTUALLY MORE LIKE A SPOOKY, SAD CRY.

SILENT FLIGHT

AT NIGHT, IT SWOOPS WITH NOISELESS WINGS.

THIS SMALL OWL IS ABOUT THE SIZE OF A ROBIN.

HIDDEN IN PLAIN SIGHT

BY DAY, IT SITS VERY STILL SO IT WON'T BE SEEN.

FARMERS' FEATHERED FRIEND

IT EATS LOTS OF MICE AND INSECTS THAT DAMAGE CROPS, BUT WILL ALSO EAT THESE THINGS:

ITS FEATHERS MAY BE REDDISH-BROWN OR GRAY.

You may not see it during the day
Or hear it when it hunts for prey,
But its ghostly cry may give you fright
When a Screech Owl calls out in the night.

Unique Small Owls

Unlike the Screech Owl, the **BURROWING OWL** is often seen during the day. It lives on the ground instead of in trees and nests in burrows, such as those once home to prairie dogs. It is found in North, Central, and South America.

ALSO KNOWN AS "GHOST OWL," SUPERSTITIOUS PEOPLE THINK THAT ITS GHOSTLY HOOT AND WAIL IS A BAD SIGN, FORTELLING DISASTERS, DISEASE, OR DEATH. ITS CRY IS REALLY A LOVE SONG.

This small owl is the only one with ear tufts. They help it look taller and scarier to enemies and help it to blend in with its surroundings as it rests by day. Its real ears are tiny holes near its eyes.

World's SMALLEST Owl

Found in the United States, it will nest in a hole in a tree or in a nest box built just for them.

At 3 weeks, the owlets will leave the nest and learn to fly. When ready, each will fly off on its own, never to return.

ELF OWL

It's the size of a HOUSE SPARROW.

This tiny owl lives in the Chihuahuan and Sonoran Deserts. It often nests in holes abandoned by woodpeckers in trees, saguaran cacti, and telephone poles.

EURASIAN JAY

THE ORIGINAL "JAY," AFTER WHICH ALL OTHER JAYS ARE NAMED. ITS CALL SOUNDS LIKE "JAY-JAY-JAY."

JAYS HELP TO PLANT NEW TREES WHEN THEY BURY ACORNS.

A JAY WILL RAISE THE FEATHERS ON ITS CROWN WHEN IT IS EXCITED.

THE EURASIAN JAY IS LARGE, NEARLY 14" (35.5 CM) LONG.

NUT COLLECTOR

WHILE IT USUALLY CARRIES ONE NUT AT A TIME, THE JAY HAS BEEN SEEN FLYING WITH UP TO FIVE NUTS AT ONCE. SOME ARE STORED IN ITS CROP.

NUTS ABOUT NUTS

JAYS EAT MOSTLY ACORNS AND OTHER NUTS, BUT WILL ALSO EAT:

BURIED TREASURE

JAYS STORE NUTS FOR THE WINTER. THEY WILL BURY NUTS IN THE GROUND AND RETURN LATER TO DIG UP THE NUTS WHEN THEY ARE HUNGRY.

A noisy jay has lots to say.
It chatters and squawks throughout the day.
One of its calls that you may hear
Is a screeching cry of "Danger's near!"

The Eurasian Jay is common across much of Europe and Asia. It lives in forests and woodlands, especially among oaks and conifers. The male and female look alike and mate for life.

Rowdy Rascal

A **BLUE JAY** is found in eastern North America. Admired for its handsome plumage, it is a familiar sight in forests and backyards. The Blue Jay can be noisy and aggressive at feeders. It also has a habit of robbing other birds' nests and eating the eggs and young birds.

Noiseless Nester

This shy bird is more often heard than seen. It is especially quiet when nesting. When a jay is hidden under cover of dense foliage, you may never notice its nest nearby.

Natural Insecticide

A jay will sit on an ant nest and allow the insects to crawl all over its fluffed-out feathers. It is believed that an acid secreted by the ants kills fleas and lice in the jay's plumage. This activity is called "anting."

Maddening Mob

A single jay can store as many as **3,000** nuts a month.

A "mob" of jays will harass a predator, such as a Tawny Owl, pestering it until it flies off. They sometimes imitate the call of another predator, such as a hawk.

Munchie Moocher

The **STELLER'S JAY** lives in forests in western North America, from Alaska to Central America. Generally shy, it can become tame when it's fed regularly. It often hangs around campgrounds and picnic areas, looking for a handout.

45

MALLARD DUCK

DUCKLINGS FOLLOW THEIR MOTHER TO WATER A DAY AFTER THEY HATCH.

LIVES IN PONDS, LAKES, OR MARSHES ALL OVER THE WORLD.

FEMALES ARE THE ONLY ONES THAT QUACK.

THE MALE HAS A SHINY GREEN HEAD AND A WHITE BAND AROUND ITS NECK.

DABBLING DUCK

DUNKING FOR FOOD IS CALLED "DABBLING."

Some ducks dive
    to the bottom of the pond
To search for food to munch.
But Mallards dabble in shallow water.
It's "bottom's up" for lunch.

DUCKS EAT WATER PLANTS AND TINY ANIMALS.

Feathers & Fluff

The Mallard female builds her nest in marsh grasses near shore. She lines it with feathers and down, which she plucks from her chest. As soon as they hatch, the ducklings know their mother by her quack.

Tricky Tree Duck

The **WOOD DUCK** is known for the male's beautiful feathers. The sharp claws on its webbed feet help it perch in trees throughout North America.

MALE

ALSO KNOWN AS **ACORN DUCK**

A WOOD DUCK WILL DUNK ONLY ITS HEAD OR PICK FOOD FROM THE WATER'S SURFACE. IT ALSO EATS SEEDS AND NUTS, ESPECIALLY ACORNS.

Preen and Clean

A duck uses its bill to straighten its feathers and coat them with a special oil from a gland near its tail for waterproofing. This process is called "preening."

Ready, Set, Drop & Plop

The Wood Duck nests in hollow trees in abandoned woodpecker holes 3 to 50 feet (1–15 m) above the ground. The female calls to the newly hatched young. One by one, they will climb out of the nest and drop to the water or ground below.

FEMALE

Duck Family Tree

Centuries ago, people used Mallards to produce a domestic breed called Pekin Duck. It was the first time ducks were raised for their meat and eggs. It's one of the most familiar cousins of the Mallard and is often seen with them in parks and on farms.

MANDARIN DUCK

ASIAN COUSIN
Possibly the Wood Duck's only rival for beauty is its relative, the Mandarin Duck, found in China.

BELTED Kingfisher

FISH FINDER

IT CAN SPOT A FISH FROM HIGH ABOVE THE WATER.

IT USES ITS LARGE BILL TO CATCH FISH AND DIG A BURROW.

KINGFISHER FEAST

IT EATS MOSTLY **FISH**, BUT IT WILL ALSO EAT:

MALE

FEMALE

PINPOINT PLUNGE

IT DIVES HEADFIRST TO SNAG ITS CATCH.

UNDERGROUND NEST

IT DIGS A BURROW IN THE BANK OF A STREAM OR RIVER.

With super sight and a spear-like bill,
This bird has earned its name.
It stares, then swoops to snatch a fish
With almost perfect aim.

Water Watcher

The odd-looking Belted Kingfisher regularly patrols waterways from southern Alaska to northern South America. Its large head and long bill seem to be too big for its body, but they are well-suited for fishing. Often spotted on a branch, utility wire, or bridge above water where it watches for fish. It may also hover in the air to spot prey, sometimes from 40 feet (12 m) high.

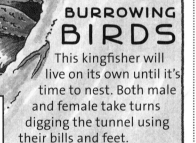

At mating time, the male gives fish to the female as a "wedding gift."

BURROWING BIRDS

This kingfisher will live on its own until it's time to nest. Both male and female take turns digging the tunnel using their bills and feet.

The nest can be more than 6 feet (2 m) from the entrance of the tunnel.

COURTEOUS KIDS

The young line up at feeding time, changing positions as they are fed, so each gets its fair share.

Dive Bomber

Like a kingfisher, a **BROWN PELICAN** dives for its prey, mainly fish. With excellent vision, it can spot a fish and dive from as high as 75 feet (23 m) above the water. It lives on the Gulf, Pacific, and Atlantic coasts of the United States.

Hilarious Hunter

The **KOOKABURRA** is an Australian crow-sized kingfisher that doesn't feed on fish. Instead, it hunts for snakes, lizards, and rodents. It's known for its crazy laughter, which has been featured in many sound tracks to jungle movies.

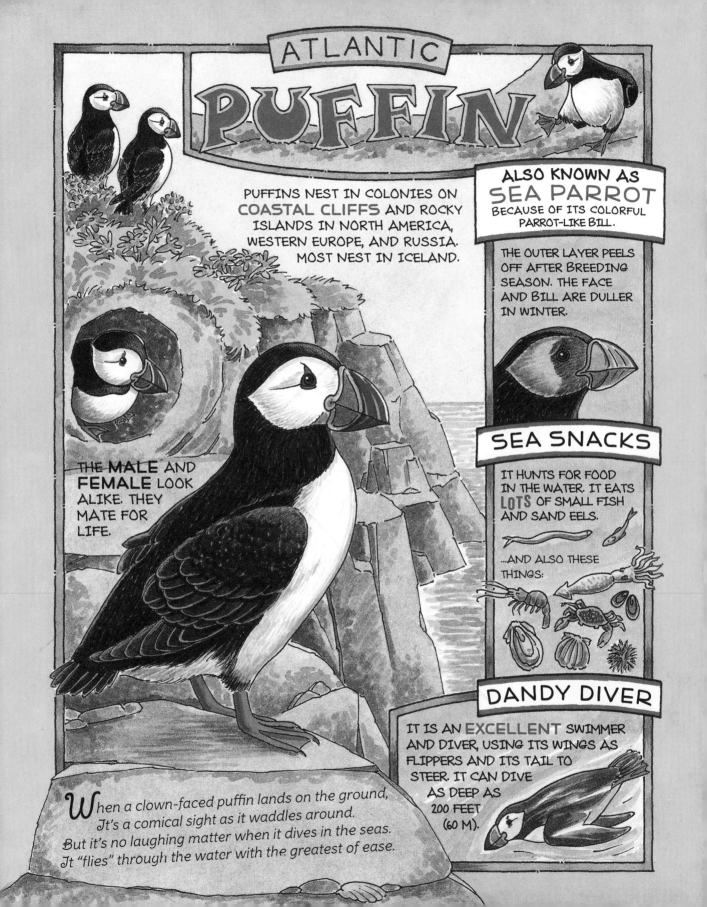

ATLANTIC PUFFIN

PUFFINS NEST IN COLONIES ON **COASTAL CLIFFS** AND ROCKY ISLANDS IN NORTH AMERICA, WESTERN EUROPE, AND RUSSIA. MOST NEST IN ICELAND.

THE **MALE** AND **FEMALE** LOOK ALIKE. THEY MATE FOR LIFE.

ALSO KNOWN AS SEA PARROT
BECAUSE OF ITS COLORFUL PARROT-LIKE BILL.

THE OUTER LAYER PEELS OFF AFTER BREEDING SEASON. THE FACE AND BILL ARE DULLER IN WINTER.

SEA SNACKS

IT HUNTS FOR FOOD IN THE WATER. IT EATS **LOTS** OF SMALL FISH AND SAND EELS.

...AND ALSO THESE THINGS:

DANDY DIVER

IT IS AN **EXCELLENT** SWIMMER AND DIVER, USING ITS WINGS AS FLIPPERS AND ITS TAIL TO STEER. IT CAN DIVE AS DEEP AS 200 FEET (60 M).

When a clown-faced puffin lands on the ground,
It's a comical sight as it waddles around.
But it's no laughing matter when it dives in the seas.
It "flies" through the water with the greatest of ease.

Dandy Diver

The Atlantic Puffin looks like a tiny penguin, but the two species are not related. They share similar traits, however: Both are skilled swimmers and divers, and both hunt underwater for food. Because they spend most of their lives in the water, they are awkward on land and leave the water only to breed. Unlike the penguin, the puffin can fly.

Bird Burrow

Puffins dig burrows for their nests in the soil of cliffs or in the crevices between rocks. The male does most of the digging, but both parents incubate, or sit on, their single egg. When the chick hatches, they feed it large quantities of small fish.

Major Mouthful

A puffin can carry as many as 10 to 30 sand eels to the nest in a single visit. It dive-bombs a school of fish and pushes each fish to the back of its mouth with its tongue. Ridges on the edges of the bill hold the fish in place.

Deepest Diver

Waddling around on land in its "tuxedo," an **EMPEROR PENGUIN**, the largest of all penguins at 4 feet (1.2 m) tall, can be an amusing sight. But in the water, this superb swimmer can dive deeper than any other bird. With a streamlined body and powerful flippers, it averages 660 feet (201 m) below the surface, but can reach 1,600 to 1,800 feet (488–549 m). Holding its breath for up to 20 minutes, it finds food, including squid, which is one of its favorites.

Frigid Father

The Emperor Penguin lives in Antarctica. It walks many miles inland on the ice to breed in the winter when the weather in the Southern Hemisphere is at its coldest. A mated pair produces a single egg. The female leaves to find food and the male incubates the egg by cradling it on top of his feet, tucking it under a warm fold of skin. He stands this way for two months, huddling with the other males in semi-darkness, in howling winds and temperatures as low as −80°F (−62°C). The female returns after the chick hatches.

The chick will spend its first several weeks riding around on its parents' feet.

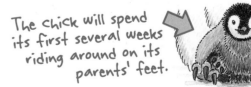

Return to the Watery World

After six weeks, the puffin parents leave their chick and go back to the sea. A week later, the chick leaves the burrow under cover of darkness and jumps off the cliff into the ocean. The chick will learn to swim, dive, fish, and fly on its own. It will not return to land for several years, when it's old enough to raise a family of its own.

Common LOON

ALSO KNOWN AS GREAT NORTHERN DIVER

IT DIVES DOWN DEEP TO FIND FOOD.

IN **SUMMER**, ITS FEATHERS ARE BLACK AND WHITE.

Loons live on the water. They build their nests at the water's edge.

IT EATS MOSTLY **FISH** BUT WILL ALSO EAT THESE THINGS:

A haunting cry and crazy laugh is the calling of a loon. It echoes 'cross the lake at dawn Or 'neath the summer moon.

IN **WINTER**, ITS FEATHERS ARE GRAY AND BROWN.

Watery World

Loons spend most of their time in the water. They sleep on the water, find food in the water, and dive beneath the surface when alarmed. They come to land only to nest.

HITCHIN' A RIDE
THE CHICKS OFTEN RIDE ON THEIR PARENTS' BACKS WHILE LEARNING TO SWIM AND DIVE.

In summer, they breed in lakes and ponds in northern North America, Greenland, and Iceland. A pair will usually have 2 chicks. The chicks take to the water soon after hatching.

Like a Loon

The **WESTERN GREBE** is a superb diver and can sink out of sight to escape its enemies. It will also carry its young on its back.

Also known as **SWAN GREBE** because of its long, thin neck.

A mating pair seem to "dance" on the water during courtship and give each other "gifts" of water weeds and algae.

Submarine Swimmer

It can hold its breath underwater for 5 minutes, while swimming for hundreds of yards or diving to 200 feet deep (61 m).

Its webbed feet are far back on its body to propel it through the water with ease, but they make it difficult to walk on land.

ARCTIC LOON

The Arctic Loon is found in high arctic regions of both hemispheres, including Scandinavia, northern Europe, and Asia. It is also known as the Black-throated Diver.

GREAT BLUE HERON

POISED LIKE A STATUE, THIS ELEGANT BIRD CAN BE SPOTTED IN BOTH FRESHWATER AND SALTWATER MARSHES, AND NEAR WATER THROUGHOUT NORTH AND CENTRAL AMERICA.

ALSO KNOWN AS

BIG CRANKY

THE HERON HAS A HARSH, CROAKING VOICE. IT LETS OUT A HUGE SQUAWK WHEN IT FEELS THREATENED.

WAIT AND WATCH

WHILE HUNTING IN SHALLOW WATER, THE BIRD USES ITS KEEN EYESIGHT TO DETECT THE SLIGHTEST MOVEMENT UNDER THE SURFACE.

STAB OR GRAB

THE HERON SNATCHES ITS PREY WITH A QUICK THRUST OF ITS POWERFUL NECK AND SPEAR-LIKE BILL.

GULP AND GONE

IT SWALLOWS WHAT IT CATCHES WHOLE. IT EATS MOSTLY FISH AND FROGS.

AT ALMOST 4 FEET TALL, IT'S THE LARGEST NORTH AMERICAN HERON.

HERON HASH

A heron is patient while hunting for prey.
It stands very still till a fish comes its way,
Or silently stalks a frog it may spy,
Then swiftly attacks in the blink of an eye.

The Great Blue Heron is easily recognized in flight, with its long neck, bill, and legs. Wings spanning 6 feet (1.8 m) help lift it into the air. Also sometimes called the Blue Crane, it is neither blue nor a crane. The Blue Heron flies with its neck tucked in, while a crane keeps its neck stretched out when it's airborne.

Fluff & Flirt

The male and female look similar. Their elaborate courtship display takes place while they build their nest high in a tree. They fluff up their feathers and strike odd poses. The male delivers sticks and branches to the female. She places each one carefully as she builds the nest.

Powder Bath

A heron cleans eel and fish slime off its feathers using "powder down." This powder is produced when the heron rubs special fragile feathers on its breast.

It combs the powder through its feathers using its bill and comb-like bristles on the middle toe of each foot.

The most abundant of the world's cranes, the **SANDHILL CRANE** is found throughout North America in freshwater wetlands, open prairies, and farmlands. One of the most ancient bird species, fossils of this bird have been found that date back 9 million years.

Cranes fly with their necks extended.

Cranes soar to great heights, so they may be difficult to spot in the sky. They gather in large flocks when they migrate, sometimes numbering in the thousands. Nearly 500,000 birds gather annually at one of their favorite rest stops along the Platte River in Nebraska.

Bird Ballet

The male and female Sandhill Cranes look alike, and the pair mates for life. Their spectacular courtship dance and musical duets are remarkable. Cranes may also dance and sing throughout the year and hundreds of birds at a time may join in. The bowing and leaping ritual has been copied by Native Americans for their ceremonies.

One of the most amazingly colored of all birds, the **GREATER FLAMINGO** is found in Africa, southern Asia, and southern Europe in saltwater coastal lagoons. Skimming its bill upside down in shallow water, the flamingo filters the water through its bill, gathering small shrimp, seeds, algae, and mollusks. Its pink color comes from some of the shrimp and algae that it eats.

HERRING GULL

NAMED FOR ITS SKILL IN CATCHING SMALL FISH SUCH AS HERRING.

ONE OF THE MOST COMMON GULLS IN NORTH AMERICA, IT IS ALSO FOUND IN GREAT BRITAIN, EUROPE, AND NORTHERN AFRICA.

CLEVER CRACKER

IT WILL DROP A CLAM ONTO ROCKS TO CRACK IT OPEN.

CLEANUP CREW

GULLS OFTEN PICK THROUGH GARBAGE, IT WILL ALSO EAT:

Flocks of Gulls help rid the beaches and waterways of garbage.

A **CHICK** WILL PECK AT THIS RED SPOT TO GET FOOD FROM ITS PARENT'S MOUTH.

Screaming, squawking, hovering, dipping,
Greedy gulls will swoop about
To grab a tasty clam or fish
Or snatch the sandwich you threw out.

A Gull Is a Gull, By Land or By Sea

Often referred to as a *seagull,* the Herring Gull spends much of its time near the sea, but it can be seen inland wherever food is found. When food is plentiful, species mix together, so it can be seen with these other gulls at various points of its range:

The **RING-BILLED GULL** looks very similar to the Herring Gull, but it is smaller and has a black band on its bill. It is found in North America and occasionally the United Kingdom.

The **GREAT BLACK-BACKED GULL**, at 30" (76 cm) long, is the world's largest gull. It can be spotted on European and Atlantic coasts and along the Great Lakes of North America.

The **LAUGHING GULL** of North and South America is known for its familiar call, which sounds like human laughter. The Herring Gull will prey on its eggs and young.

Pretty in Pink

Scientists have studied Herring Gull colonies by tracking birds they have sprayed with brightly colored dyes. A pink gull may look bizarre to humans, but the other gulls in the flock seem to see nothing odd.

Beach Buddy

Gulls share the shoreline with other birds, such as the **SANDERLING**. While it breeds in the Arctic, this small sandpiper is found on almost any sandy beach in the world. It races back and forth with the waves and probes for food in the sand as the water recedes.

A statue of two gulls sits on top of the monument.

The Gull That Saved Utah

In Salt Lake City, Utah, a monument honors the California Gull's role in saving Mormon settlers' crops from a grasshopper plague in 1848. It is the state bird of Utah. It lives along the Pacific coast and in the interior of western North America.

ARE YOU MY MOTHER?
AS THE CHICKS GROW, THEY WILL WANDER AWAY FROM THE NEST. THE ADULTS CAN FIND AND RECOGNIZE THEIR YOUNG, BUT THE CHICK MAY NOT RECOGNIZE ITS PARENT AND WILL BEG FOR FOOD FROM ANY ADULT.

Red-winged Blackbird

FOUND IN MARSHES, SWAMPS, AND WET AND DRY MEADOWS IN NORTH AND CENTRAL AMERICA

FEMALE

FEATHERED FRIENDS

IN WINTER, IT GATHERS IN **HUGE** FLOCKS WITH OTHER BIRDS.

WOVEN WONDER

IT WEAVES A STURDY NEST BETWEEN STEMS OF WATER PLANTS.

MALE

HE FLASHES HIS RED SHOULDER PATCHES TO ATTRACT A MATE AND KEEP OTHER MALES AWAY.

This blackbird comes to the marsh in spring.
He finds a perch and starts to sing.
He sings to claim a place to nest
And tell the females, "I'm the best."

Sneaky Search

The male Red-winged Blackbird can hide his red feathers when he searches for food in another bird's territory.

It eats mostly insects, as many as a **TRILLION** a year. But it also eats lots of seeds and grain.

FLOCK & FEED

IN LATE SUMMER, SOME RED-WINGED BLACKBIRDS GATHER IN HUGE FLOCKS WITH GRACKLES, COWBIRDS, AND STARLINGS. THEY FORAGE ON THE GROUND FOR INSECTS AND SEEDS. AS WINTER APPROACHES AND THEY BEGIN TO FLY SOUTH, THE FLOCKS GROW IN NUMBERS, SOMETIMES IN THE MILLIONS.

"Flock Mate"

The Purple Grackle

The large **COMMON GRACKLE** is a bird that often flocks with blackbirds. It is found in eastern North America and comes in two varients: purple and bronzed. Though it looks black from a distance, its feathers shimmer in glossy blue, purple, bronze, and green.

Bad Breeding Habits

Two other birds often join flocks of blackbirds. They have reputations for certain anti-social behaviors toward other birds.

FEMALE

MALE

The female **BROWN-HEADED COWBIRD** lays its eggs in nests of songbirds, leaving them to hatch and be raised by foster bird parents. The larger Cowbird nestling pushes the others out of the nest or manages to get most of the food offered by the parents.

The **STARLING**, originally found in Europe, Africa, and Asia, has been introduced to many other countries, where it has flourished. It is very aggressive during breeding season. It forces native birds, especially bluebirds and woodpeckers, out of their nests and uses the nesting sites for itself.

The Bronzed Grackle

The feathers shimmer in the light.

Like the Red-winged Blackbird, this male grackle performs a courtship display of puffing out his feathers while he sings to attract a mate.

Canada Goose

IN THE **FALL**, SOME FLY SOUTH FOR THE WINTER. OTHERS REMAIN IN THE NORTH ALL YEAR ROUND.

THE **FLOCK** FLIES IN A "**V**" SHAPE WHEN MIGRATING.

THE MALE IS CALLED A **GANDER**. THE FEMALE IS CALLED A **GOOSE**. THEY LOOK ALIKE.

FUZZY FAMILY

THE BABIES HATCH IN SPRING. THEY ARE CALLED **GOSLINGS**.

SPRING SWIM

THE GOSLINGS FOLLOW THEIR PARENTS TO WATER SOON AFTER THEY HATCH.

High up in the autumn sky, Canada Geese are flying by. Their noisy honking that you hear Means that winter days are near.

Familiar Flyer

Well known across North America, the Canada Goose breeds in Canada and in much of the United States. It may migrate as far south as Mexico in winter. A strong flyer, it can reach speeds of more than 40 miles (64 km) per hour.

FLYING WEDGE

The V-shape formation serves two purposes. (1) The birds save energy this way. As each bird flaps its wings, that breaks the wind for the one behind it, which makes flying easier. The leader has the hardest job, so the birds take turns being in front. (2) The V shape allows them to maintain eye contact, so the flock stays together.

Flocks of Double-crested Cormorants also fly in a V shape.

KEEP AWAY!

Canada Geese mate for life. The gander will guard his goose, fiercely defending their nest, and may attack if an intruder gets too close.

Green Grazers

IT EATS GRASSES, ROOTS, AND WATER PLANTS, BUT IT WILL ALSO EAT:

Beautiful Bullies

A native of Europe and Asia, the **MUTE SWAN** has been introduced in other countries for its beauty.

SWAN SONG LEGEND SAYS THAT SWANS WILL SING A SPECIAL SONG RIGHT BEFORE THEY DIE. THE MUTE SWAN IS NOT WITHOUT A VOICE, BUT NEITHER DOES IT SING. IT'S MOSTLY SILENT, BUT WILL GRUNT OR HISS.

Like Canada Geese, a pair of Mute Swans will mate for life. They will attack intruders to their nesting territory, including humans and other swans. One pair will live in and defend their pond or stretch of stream for their entire lives.

ISLAND EVOLUTION

The **NENE** is the state bird of Hawaii, the only place it lives in the wild. It evolved from the Canada Goose, but its feet have less webbing and are better suited to walking on the dry mountainside of the Big Island and Maui.

Northern Mockingbird

MOONLIGHT SERENADE

MALES DO MOST OF THE SINGING AND WILL SING BOTH DAY AND NIGHT. MOST OF THE NIGHT SINGERS ARE MALES WITHOUT MATES, AND THEY ARE MOST COMMONLY HEARD DURING THE FULL MOON.

IT IS FOUND IN MANY HABITATS INCLUDING OPEN COUNTRY WITH THICKETS AND DESERT BRUSHLANDS.

A FAVORITE SONGBIRD THROUGH-OUT NORTH AMERICA, IT HAS BEEN CHOSEN BY FIVE STATES AS THEIR OFFICIAL BIRD.

THE **MALE** AND **FEMALE** LOOK SIMILAR.

MATING MELODIES

DURING COURTSHIP, A MALE MAY FLUTTER HIGH IN THE AIR WHILE POURING OUT HIS SONG.

DESERT DIGS

IT BUILDS A NEST IN A CACTUS OR SAGEBRUSH.

Crickets, a chicken,
and a barking dog,
Sirens and whistles, and a croaking frog,
These are some sounds that you
may hear
When a mimicking mockingbird is near.

IT EATS INSECTS. IN THE DESERT, IT ALSO FEEDS ON BERRIES SUCH AS MISTLETOE AND FRUITS OF YUCCA AND CACTI.

Also known as the Mimic Thrush, the Northern Mockingbird lives up to its name by being able to imitate up to 35 bird species. It copies other sounds as well, including animals, machines, piano notes, and the human voice. Some of its songs are a blend of its own melodies and copied sounds, but mimicry is only about 10 percent of its total song output. It may learn up to 200 songs in its lifetime. The more songs a male knows, the more attractive he is to a female.

Wing Flash

The flash of its white wing patches, unmistakable in flight, is also its way to communicate aggression toward predators and attraction toward a female. While foraging for food on the ground, it jerks its wings over its back. The wing flashing may serve to scare up insects.

Aggressive Attacker

A mostly solitary bird, except when breeding, it is strongly territorial and will attack anything it sees as a threat to its nesting site. It will dive-bomb rattlesnakes, hawks, cats, dogs, and humans, screaming a loud "CHACK!" which means, "Don't come near!" It will even attack its own reflection, sometimes so viciously, that it may harm or even kill itself.

The **CURVED-BILL THRASHER** is a cousin of the mockingbird and is found in North America, mainly in the Southwest. It favors dry desert brushland and areas with cacti.

Skillful Songster

Although the Curved-bill Thrasher is less talented at mimicry than the mockingbird, its song is just as sweet. It's commonly seen and heard calling loudly from atop a tall cactus. The call sounds like human whistling.

Thrash and Feed

Named for its feeding habit of thrashing its head from side to side while it forages on the ground, it uses its long, curved bill to dig up insects. It also feeds on nectar from agave and the fruit of cacti.

Spiny Shelter

Nesting in a cactus or a thorny bush, it is easily seen, but protected by the plant's pointy spines. The male and female look alike.

This silky-flycatcher inhabits North and Central American deserts. The Phainopepla's' song is not as complex as the mockingbird's but it does include imitations of many species of birds. While it mainly eats insects, which it can catch in the air, it also eats berries and other small fruits.

PHAINOPEPLA

THE FASTEST RUNNER OF BIRDS THAT FLY, THE ROADRUNNER CAN SPRINT UP TO 25 MPH (40 KMPH).

ALSO KNOWN AS **CHAPARRAL COCK**

GREATER Roadrunner

CHAPARRAL IS A DENSE THICKET OF SCRUBBY PLANTS IN THE HOT, DRY FOOTHILLS OF THE SOUTHWESTERN UNITED STATES AND MEXICO.

IT RAISES ITS CREST WHEN EXCITED.

A FLEXIBLE TAIL HELPS THE ROADRUNNER STEER THROUGH CACTUS AND BRUSH.

HAVING TWO TOES IN FRONT AND TWO TOES IN BACK MAY HELP THE ROADRUNNER MAINTAIN ITS BALANCE.

GIFTS OF LOVE

DURING COURTSHIP, THE MALE WILL OFFER A TWIG TO THE FEMALE TO SAY, "LET'S BUILD A NEST."

LATER HE'LL BRING HER A LIZARD OR A SNAKE TO SAY, "LET'S RAISE A FAMILY." REPTILES ARE THE MAIN FOOD BROUGHT FOR NESTLINGS.

PRICKLY PAD

THE NEST IS BUILT IN A CACTUS OR A BUSH.

DASH & DART FOR DINNER

IT CHASES DOWN ITS PREY, MAINLY INSECTS, BUT IT ALSO EATS:

Though a roadrunner walks with an awkward step,
Its predators find that it's hard to catch.
Built for speed, it can sprint away.
Among birds that fly, it has no match.

The Greater Roadrunner is a cuckoo that runs on the ground. It's crow-sized, about 9" (23 cm) tall and 2 feet (61 cm) long. The sexes look similar, but the male is larger. Some think its common name of *roadrunner* comes from stalking heat-seeking lizards on paved roads. But Mexicans called it *corre camino,* meaning "it runs the road," long before modern highways. The birds follow animal trails to search for food.

Smart Sunbather

Well adapted to the desert's hot days that cool down 50°F (10°C) or more at night, it will conserve energy by lowering its own body temperature as much as 7°F (-14°C). At sunrise, it turns its back to the sun and lifts up its feathers to expose a dark patch of skin that acts as a solar panel. This raises its temperature to normal without using its own energy.

ALSO KNOWN AS "SNAKE KILLER"

A roadrunner won't hesitate to kill a rattlesnake for food. It darts at the snake to make it strike, then pecks at its eyes and head until the snake is dead. Unlike other prey, the snake is too long for the roadrunner to swallow whole, so part of the snake will dangle out of its mouth. The roadrunner swallows it bit by bit, as the lower end is digested.

Eat and Be Eaten

Roadrunner meat is sometimes eaten in Mexico. Because of the bird's ability to digest poisonous animals without harm, some folk healers recommend "roadrunner stew" to cure a number of illnesses.

Ultra Bird
OSTRICHES

are extraordinary. The fastest runner among flightless birds, an ostrich can reach speeds of up to 45 mph (72 kmph) to escape its enemies. It has been found in the African savanna and desert for thousands of years. A giant among birds, it is the tallest at 9 feet (3 m) and can weigh up to 330 pounds (150 kg).

MALE

Speedy Toes

Its feet have only two toes, which is thought to reduce friction while running. They are hoof-like and similar to the feet of many grazing mammals. It eats grasses, seeds, fruits, and flowers.

FEMALE

The More the Merrier

A dominant male has a "harem" of two to five females, called hens. The "major hen" is the first to lay eggs after she scrapes out a hollow in the ground. She lays up to 12 eggs. "Minor hens," which have mated with other males, are invited to lay eggs in the same nest. The record for the most eggs in one nest is 80. The major hen and the male share incubating duties.

EGGSTREME EGGS

An ostrich lays the biggest egg of any bird. At 6–8" (15–20 cm) long, it can weigh more than 3 pounds (1.4 kg). It takes 40 minutes to hard-boil.

Ostrich

Chicken

Anna's Hummingbird

THE MOST COMMON HUMMINGBIRD ON THE WEST COAST OF NORTH AMERICA, IT DOES NOT MIGRATE AND CAN BE FOUND IN SEMI-DESERT HABITATS ALL YEAR.

KNOWN FOR THEIR JEWEL-LIKE FEATHERS, A FLOCK OF HUMMERS IS SOMETIMES CALLED A "GLITTERING" OR A "SHIMMER."

MALE HUMMINGBIRDS HAVE AN IRIDESCENT THROAT PATCH. THE MALE ANNA'S HUMMINGBIRD ALSO HAS THESE SHINY FEATHERS ON HIS CROWN.

WHIRRING WINGS

HUMMERS HAVE THE FASTEST WING BEATS OF ANY BIRD, UP TO 80 PER SECOND. THEY MOVE THEIR WINGS IN THE SHAPE OF A FIGURE EIGHT, MAKING A HUMMING SOUND.

FLOWER FAVOR

HUMMERS HELP POLLINATE FLOWERS AS THEY FLIT FROM BLOOM TO BLOOM. THEY TRANSFER POLLEN ON THEIR HEADS AND BILLS. THEY ARE OFTEN ATTRACTED TO RED FLOWERS:

OCOTILLO

MONKEY FLOWER

HEDGEHOG CACTUS

CALIFORNIA FUCHSIA

FEEDING CONTINUOUSLY THROUGHOUT THE DAY, IT MUST EAT ALMOST TWICE ITS BODY WEIGHT IN FOOD.

CONSTANTLY IN MOTION, IT PERCHES ONLY BRIEFLY TO REST AND SURVEY ITS SURROUNDINGS. WITH VERY SMALL FEET AND LEGS, IT CAN'T WALK, BUT IT CAN SCOOT SIDEWAYS ON A PERCH.

ON THE GO

SWEET SIPPER

WITH ITS LONG BILL AND TONGUE FORKED WITH FUZZY TIPS, IT CAN PROBE DEEPLY INTO A FLOWER TO LAP UP ITS NECTAR.

Forward, backward, up and down,
A hummingbird will zip and zoom,
Then hover at its favorite flowers
To sip the nectar from each bloom.

THE FEMALE HAS JUST A TINY THROAT PATCH.

Hummingbirds are found only in the Americas. Some of the smallest birds, they are no larger than a ping-pong ball and no heavier than a nickel. When hummers were first encountered by European settlers, the newcomers wondered if these tiny creatures were a cross between a bird and an insect. The settlers sometimes called them "flybirds." Anna's Hummingbird is less than 4" (10 cm) long. It is found in a wide range of habitats, including the desert, where it is one of the earliest nesters in February or March.

The only hummer that breeds in eastern North America, the **RUBY-THROATED HUMMINGBIRD** is named for its red throat patch. These birds are found in open woodland, suburbs, and parks, and are regular visitors at backyard feeders. In addition to the nectar they get from flowers, the sugar water in hummingbird feeders is a good source of the fuel for these creatures. They need this energy for their long migration before winter. These tiny birds will travel south for 1,850 miles (2,977 km), including a 500-mile (805-km) nonstop flight over the Gulf of Mexico, to reach Mexico and Central America.

Daredevil Dive

The male Anna's performs a courtship display of high-speed plunges from 130 feet (40 m) in the air. As he reaches a perching female, he pulls up, producing an explosive "pop" with his tail feathers. Unlike most other hummers, he sings a squeaky song during courtship.

Cradle Cup

The female builds the nest by spreading her sticky saliva on a twig to make a tiny platform. She constructs the nest around her with plant down, spiderwebs, moss, and lichens, a perfect cup about 2" (5 cm) in diameter.

Tiny & Tidy

The female builds a cup-shaped nest in a tree or shrub using plant down and spiderwebs. The nest is only 1" (2.5 cm) tall by 1 1/2" (3.8 cm) wide. She lays two coffee bean-sized eggs. When they hatch, the nestlings are no larger than honeybees. The nest can expand as they grow because of the stretchy spider silk holding it together.

Found only on the island of Cuba, this is the world's tiniest bird. It is 2 1/4" (5.7 cm) long and weighs no more than two paper clips. It probably has the smallest eggs at 1/2" by 1/3" (13 x 8 mm). It would take 3,000 of its eggs to equal the weight of the egg of an ostrich, the world's largest bird.

BEE HUMMINGBIRD

Seeking Seeping Sugar

Like all hummers, the Anna's main food is nectar, as well as small insects and spiders. This species will also visit the holes drilled by a sapsucker (a kind of woodpecker) in a living tree. Hummingbirds will lap up the seeping sap and pluck the insects that are attracted to it.

GILA WOODPECKER

Pronounced "HEE-luh," it is named for the Gila River in Arizona and New Mexico.

ITS WHITE WING PATCHES CAN BE SEEN WHEN IT FLIES.

THE **MALE** HAS A CAP OF RED FEATHERS ON THE TOP OF HIS HEAD.

IT USES ITS LONG, POINTED BILL TO DIG OUT A NEST HOLE AND PROBE FOR INSECTS. IT LAPS THEM UP WITH ITS LONG, STICKY TONGUE.

A single Giant Saguaro may have many woodpecker holes in it.

HOME, PRICKLY HOME

IT BUILDS A NEST IN A HOLE IN A TREE OR A SAGUARO CACTUS. THE CACTUS IS IDEAL BECAUSE THE SPINES KEEP PREDATORS OUT AND IT IS A COOL SHELTER IN THE DESERT.

FEMALE

HUNGRY GILA

IT EATS MAINLY **INSECTS** BUT WILL ALSO SIP SUGAR WATER FROM HUMMINGBIRD FEEDERS AND EAT THESE THINGS:

CACTUS FRUIT

IT HELPS TO POLLINATE THE FLOWERS OF THE SAGUARO CACTUS AS IT SIPS THE SWEET NECTAR INSIDE.

Pecking and digging between the spines,
A woodpecker slurps up the insects it finds.
It chisels in deeper to carve out a nest.
As a safe place for young ones, a cactus is best.

The Gila Woodpecker is found in deserts and brushy woodlands of North America, especially in Saguaro Cactus forests. Unlike most wood-peckers, the Gila Woodpecker thrives in the desert with almost no trees. The Giant Saguaro provides food and shelter.

Gila Healer

This woodpecker helps to protect the cactus from disease by eating the damaging insects inside it. As it digs out the insect larvae, it also cuts away the diseased parts of the plant. As the sap hardens, the cactus is healed.

COZY CAVITY

AFTER HOLLOWING OUT THE CACTUS FOR THE NEST, A PAIR OF MALE AND FEMALE GILA WOODPECKERS WAIT FOR THE SAP TO DRY BEFORE MOVING IN.

The cavity becomes a sturdy, waterproof structure called a "boot."

When the cactus dies and decays, the boot remains and may become a shelter for a critter on the ground.

Need a Nest?

A pair of woodpeckers will reuse their nest from year to year. When abandoned, other animals move in and make it a home. This includes **ELF OWLS** and other birds, rodents, and reptiles.

The **GILDED FLICKER** is another woodpecker that lives in the deserts of North America and uses the Saguaro Cactus as a nesting site. Unlike most woodpeckers, a flicker forages mainly on the ground for insects (mostly ants), berries, and cactus fruit.

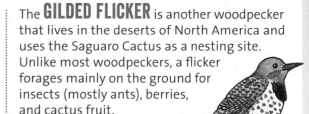

Flashing Yellow

The Gilded Flicker is similar to the more-widespread **NORTHERN FLICKER**. The Gilded has a separate range and has adapted to the desert, where the Northern never breeds. The Gilded looks like a cross between the Northern Flicker of the East with yellow under-wings, and the Northern Flicker of the West (shown below) with a red mustache.

Ant Antics

The flicker's favorite food is ants, which may be half its diet. Using its long, sticky tongue to reach deep into an anthill, it is immune to the harmful acid secreted by ants. When not eating them, it will take advantage of that acid by performing "anting" behavior. That is, it will let the ants crawl all over its feathers. The ants' acid may kill lice and other parasites and help to keep the bird clean.

There are no woodpeckers in Australia, but the most similar are the treecreepers. The White-Browed Tree-creeper is found in the mulga woodlands of the deserts.

WHITE-BROWED TREECREEPER

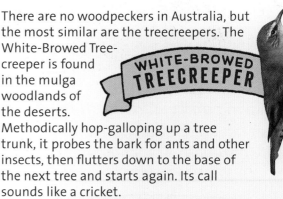

Methodically hop-galloping up a tree trunk, it probes the bark for ants and other insects, then flutters down to the base of the next tree and starts again. Its call sounds like a cricket.

The California Quail is found in western North America in woodlands, sagebrush, chaparral, and desert. It has been introduced as a game bird in Australia, New Zealand, and Chile.

Airbound Burst

This plump and handsome ground dweller would rather walk than fly. But with powerful wings it can fly short distances to escape danger.

Fowl Family

Both parents share incubation in the shallow nest on the ground. Both will also care for the young. Looking like fuzzy wind-up toys, the chicks will follow their parents around soon after they hatch, learning to feed themselves.

Daily Dust Bath

A quail will wriggle around in soft soil, using its body to dig out a shallow "bathtub." Flapping and ruffling, it will spread the dust throughout its feathers. This method of grooming cleans the feathers and removes parasites.

CHUKAR

The Chukar is a partridge native to Eurasia. It has been introduced in North America and New Zealand as a game bird. Its name comes from its call.

Like the quail, the
GREATER SAGE-GROUSE
is in the family of "chicken-like" birds. The largest grouse in North America, it is found in western scrubby areas and sagebrush. Named for its habitat and main food of sage, this grouse is becoming less common as humans take over the sagebrush plains.

SECLUDED IN SAGE

The female builds her nest under cover of sagebrush, lining it with grasses and sagebrush leaves. She incubates and raises the young without the male's help.

ALSO KNOWN AS
Cock of the Plains

The males gather for a dramatic courtship ritual at a "lek," an open area where they strut, bow, and display their plumage to try to impress the females. As many as 60 males will participate, but only a few will be chosen by the females. The most stunning part of the display is when the male puffs out his chest feathers, inflates two air sacs on his chest, and then releases them, producing a popping sound like a cork being pulled from a bottle. The "drumming" and strutting is repeated for hours and can go on for weeks.

The Harris's Hawk is found in deserts and scrubland in North, Central, and South America. One of its former names was "One-banded Buzzard" for the broad, white band at the base of its tail.

Sociable birds, they are unique in that they live together in family groups, hunt together, and share the catch.

The very common **TURKEY VULTURE** is found mainly near woods, but also in the deserts of North, South, and Central America. This large bird is named for its similarity to a Wild Turkey, with its bald red head and dark body. The word *vulture* comes from a Latin word meaning "to pluck or tear." Like the Harris's Hawk, it tears its food apart with its hooked beak.

Feathered Family

The female builds a nest of sticks in trees, bushes, and cacti. She may share it with her mate and a few other males and females, usually their young that hatched in previous years. Each adult will help incubate the eggs and will share in feeding the young. This family group provides more protection for the young from predators.

Greasy Grimy Guts

A vulture's main food is dead animals, which it finds with its extremely keen sense of smell. It doesn't like to share its stinky meal and will threaten an intruder with a hiss or a grunt, the only noise it makes. If it's really annoyed, it will throw up on the other bird, an action also used in self-defense if it is frightened.

Temperature Control

You may see them perching with their wings spread, usually in the morning, to warm up or dry off in the sun. They also do this to cool off on hot days, as the open wings release heat. They may also pee on their legs to cool down.

Happy Hunters

The Harris's Hawk is one of the most popular in falconry, where hunters use this bird of prey to catch small animals. About the size of a crow, it is often considered a "beginner's bird," because it's easy to train. Harris's Hawks have been used in European towns to scare off bird pests, such as pigeons and starlings.

JUVENILE

This large raptor is found in a variety of remote habitats, including deserts in North America, Europe, parts of Africa, and Asia. It is one of the largest raptors and can reach speeds of 150 to 200 mph (241–322 kmph) when diving for prey. It eats anything it can kill, including other large birds of prey.

GOLDEN EAGLE

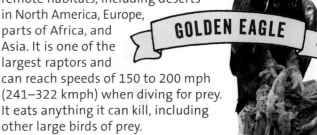

GLOSSARY

abdomen belly

arid very dry, as in a desert habitat

asymmetrical not the same on both sides, as in the ear placement of some owls

beak the shorter, hooked bill of a raptor or parrot

bill the jaws of a bird, including their horny covering

bon voyage a French phrase, usually translated as "Have a nice trip"

boring making a hole in something

bristles short, stiff hairs

breed *(verb)* to pair animals, such as birds, to produce offspring

brood the young birds hatched from a group of eggs in a single nest, usually laid by one female

burrows holes or tunnels dug by an animal to live in

canopy the highest layer of overlapping branches in a group of trees in a forest or woodland

captivity in reference to birds, kept as a pet in a cage

carcass the body of a dead animal

cavity a hollow space, often used for a nest

chisel *(verb)* to cut into or chip away at something

cooing the low, soft cry of a bird

courting ritual an activity that leads to mating

crest the showy growth of feathers on the head of a bird

crop a saclike area beneath the throat used to store undigested food

cross-breed *(verb)* to pair different birds to produce offspring with desired traits of each bird

crown the top of the head of a bird

dominant in birds, the biggest or most important bird(s) in a group

down *(feather)* soft, fluffy feathers on a young bird or the layers of insulating feathers beneath an adult's outer feathers

down *(plant)* the fuzzy fluff on some seeds that a bird may use to line its nest

duet a song or call that two birds do together

evolve to change

fledgling a young bird that has grown its first complete set of flight feathers and has left the nest

flippers a broad, flat limb used for swimming

forage to search for food

fossil an imprint of a plant or animal from a past age preserved in earth or rock

gizzard the large part of the bird's digestive system, where food is ground into small pieces

gland a part of the body that produces a substance for a particular purpose, such as oil for waterproofing a bird's feathers

hatch to emerge from an egg

hover to hang in the air on fluttering wings

incubate to sit on eggs to hatch them by warmth

lagoons shallow ponds or channels

larvae the young, wingless form of many insects

lichens plantlike living things that grow on solid surfaces

mate (noun) a bird's chosen partner with which it wants to start a family

mating the process by which a pair of birds join together to produce offspring

migrate to move from one region to another, often on a regular schedule for feeding or breeding

native originally found in a particular country

nestling a young bird that has not yet left the nest

parasite an animal or plant that lives on or in another to feed off its host

pellet material that cannot be digested and was thrown up by a bird of prey

plumage the term for all of the feathers that cover a bird's body

pollen a mass of tiny particles in a flower that fertilize the seeds

pollinate to transfer pollen from one flower to another

predator an animal that lives by killing and eating other animals

puncture to make a hole with a point

raptor a bird of prey that kills and eats other animals; it usually has keen eyesight, a hooked beak, and sharp talons

rodent a small mammal that uses its sharp front teeth for gnawing

savanna grasslands with a scattering of trees or shrubs

scavenger an animal that feeds on dead matter

sprint to run at full speed, especially for a short distance

suet hard animal fat

talon the claw of a bird of prey

terrestrial relating to the land

twitter to make a series of chirping noises

webbed as in feet, having skin that connects the toes of some water birds, such as ducks

whirring to fly or move rapidly with a buzzing sound

BIBLIOGRAPHY

BOOKS

Alderfer, Jonathan, and Paul Hess. *National Geographic Backyard Guide to the Birds of North America*. Washington, D.C.: National Geographic Society, 2011.

Alderton, David. *The Complete Illustrated Encyclopedia of Birds of the World*. Leicestershire, UK: Lorenz Books, 2012.

Audubon/Birdlife International. *Bird: The Definitive Visual Guide*. New York: DK Publishing, 2009.

Beletsky, Les. *Birds of the World*. Baltimore: Johns Hopkins University Press, 2006.

Bradbury, Will. *Birds of Sea, Shore & Stream*. Time-Life Films. Inc., 1976.

Brinkley, Edward S. *National Wildlife Federation Field Guide to Birds of North America*. New York: Sterling Publishing Co., Inc., 2007.

Bull , John, and John Farrand, Jr. *The Audubon Society Field Guide to North American Birds, Eastern Region*. New York: Alfred A. Knopf, 1977.

Collins, Henry Hill, Jr., and Ned R. Boyajian. *Familiar Garden Birds of America*. New York: Harper & Row, Publishers, 1965.

Couzens, Dominic. *Extreme Birds*. New York: Firefly Books, Ltd., HarperCollins, 2011.

Durrell, Gerald, with Lee Durrell. *The Amateur Naturalist*. New York: Alfred A. Knopf, 1983.

Forbush, Edward Howe, and John Bichard May. *A Natural History of American Birds of Eastern and Central North America*. Boston: Houghton Mifflin Company, 1939.

Goodfellow, Peter. *Birds as Builders*. New York: Arco Publishing Company, Inc., 1977.

Hanzak, J. *The Pictorial Encyclopedia of Birds*. London: Hamlyn Publishing Group Ltd., 1965.

Koch, Maryjo. *Bird, Egg, Feather, Nest*. New York: Stewart, Tabori & Chang, 1992.

Lemmon, Robert S. *Our Amazing Birds*. New York: Doubleday & Company, Inc., 1952.

Line, Les, and Franklin Russell. *The Audubon Society Book of Wild Birds*. New York: Harry N. Abrams, Inc., Publishers, 1976.

Menaboni, Athos and Sara. *Menaboni's Birds*. New York: Rinehart & Company, Inc., 1950.

Peterson, Roger Tory. *Life Nature Library: The Birds*. New York: Time Inc., 1963.

Reader's Digest. *Marvels & Mysteries of Our Animal World*. New York: Coronet Books, 1964.

———. *Birds: Their Life, Their Ways, Their World*. New York: Reader's Digest Association, Inc., 1979.

———. *Nature in America*. New York: Reader's Digest Association, Inc., 1991.

Schneck, Marcus. *Garden Bird Facts*. London: Quarto Publishing, 1992.

Sibley, David Allen. *The Sibley Guide to Birds: National Audubon Society*. New York: Alfred A. Knopf, 2000.

Tekiela, Stan, and Karen Shanberg. *Nature Smart: A Family Guide to Nature, Midwest & Eastern*. Minnesota: Adventure Publications, 1995.

MAGAZINES

National Wildlife Federation. *Ranger Rick*® magazine. Reston, Va.

National Geographic Society. *National Geographic* magazine. Washington, D.C.

WEBSITES

All About Birds — Cornell Lab of Ornithology: www.allaboutbirds.org

Arizona-Sonora Desert Museum: www.desertmuseum.org

Birding Information: www.birdinginformation.com

The Nature Conservancy: www.nature.org

National Audubon Society Birds: birds.audubon.org

National Wildlife Federation: www.nwf.org

ACKNOWLEDGEMENTS

The joy of discovery in nature has always been a part of my work as an artist. I feel privileged to share it others in this book, my first. As it is a dream come true for me, I would like to thank those who had a hand in making it happen. The seed for this project was planted many years ago as I created a book which was very similar to this in concept and design, but the focus was "wildflowers." It fell into the lap of Kim Kerin, then Art Director at National Wildlife Federation's *Your Big Backyard* magazine. She recognized the unique creative vision and proposed a monthly series featuring wildflowers, as well as other subjects that kids would enjoy. Under her guidance and the input of the editor, Mary Dalheim, and subsequent editor, Lori Collins, and designer, Megan Isom Smith, the series flourished in the magazine for many years. When the column had run its course, I had a collection of 94 pages which I felt was destined to become a book.

A friend and colleague, Greg Oviatt, saw the value of the collection and got on board as my agent, providing valuable advice about creating a book proposal. He then picked up the ball and ran with it, making connections and handing it off to J.P. Leventhal, publisher at Black Dog & Leventhal, who saw the magic and felt compelled to continue the dream. Filling the pages to create this first book has been a monumental task, a big puzzle, as Dinah Dunn, my editor at BD&L, would say. She had the extreme organizational skills to make the pieces fit and the unbridled enthusiasm to keep the ball rolling. Carol Bobolts, of Red Herring Design, contributed intuitive design in her layouts that complemented my own. Ellen Lambeth, Executive Editor at NWF's *Ranger Rick* magazine, provided expertise to tweak the details as we completed the work. Brianna Tom and Julie Blessyn at NWF and numerous other individuals also helped to bring this to fruition.

Many friends and family members have cheered me on from the sidelines. A special thank you to my best friend, Dana Stewart, who supported me with unlimited positive energy and comic relief, not to mention providing many bird books and keeping me fed. I offer my heartfelt appreciation to all of these wonderful folks as my dream has become a reality. And I am grateful to be able to share my "sense of wonder" about our natural world, which is the inspiration for it all.